Clever and Quirky Creatures

Rob Morrison

Contents

ETA
Cuisenaire

Introduction

Nobody knows quite how many different types of animals there are in the world. People who study animals are called **zoologists**. They sort animals into groups. Each group is called a phylum (say *file-um*). There's a **phylum** for animals with backbones; there's another phylum for animals with skeletons outside their bodies, and so on.

The animal groups may be different, but they are related. Zoologists believe that one group developed from another, each more advanced than the one from which it grew. It is like a "tree" with branches, or groups, that grow upward and outward. You can see the Animal Relationships Tree on page 22.

Zoologists know a lot about animal groups—but there are amazing animal facts that even some zoologists don't know! So read on...and be amazed!

Real No-Brainers

Sponges might look like plants, but they are really animals.

Sponges are the simplest of all animals. For many years, people thought that sponges were plants because they *looked* like plants. But sponges catch their own food, like all animals. Sponges belong to the phylum called *Porifera* (say *por-if-er-a*).

A sponge has no head, no brain, and no nervous system. So, how does it live? Sponges have thousands of little holes in their sides. They draw in water through these holes, then blow it out through a large hole at the top. Sponges remove tiny plants and animals, called **plankton**, from the water as it passes through their bodies. Plankton is their only food.

Sponge Soup!

Sponges might not have brains—but some of them can do a very impressive trick! If you squash a sponge through a cloth, so that it is separated into a soupy mix, it can put itself back together again cell by cell.

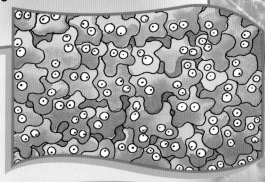

Common Name	Scientific Name
sponges	*Porifera*

Wobblers

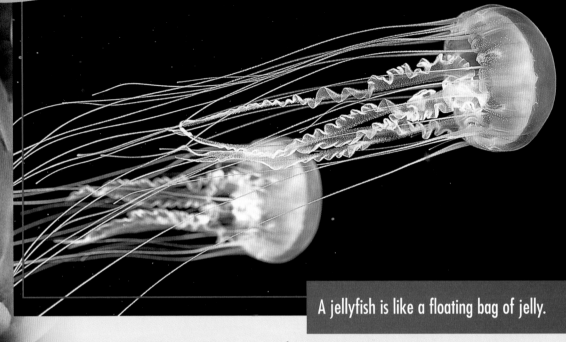

A jellyfish is like a floating bag of jelly.

Imagine you have a clear bag of jelly. Now put tentacles around the bag and turn it upside down. Your bag of jelly has just become a jellyfish.

The opening of the bag is like the jellyfish's mouth. It uses the drooping **tentacles** around its mouth to sting and paralyse sea creatures. Then it uses the tentacles to take the food to its mouth.

Don't be spineless! Stand up for yourself!

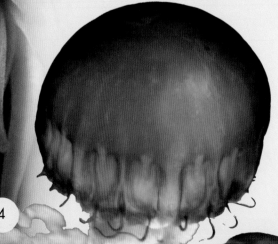

Upside-Down Jellyfish

Now turn the jellyfish so that its opening faces upward. It looks like a **sea anemone**, which feeds as a jellyfish does.

Sea anemones and jellyfish belong to the phylum of *Coelenterates* (say *seel-en-ter-ates*). The stinging cells in their tentacles contain some of nature's strongest poisons.

A sea anemone's mouth and tentacles point upward. An anemone's tentacles fire their poison when they are touched by another animal.

But some animals do not set off an anemone's poison; instead, they hide in the anemone's tentacles, where they are safe from **predators**.

A few animals actually eat anemones. Instead of being poisoned, these animals build the stinging cells into their bodies for their own defense.

A sea anemone is like an upside-down jellyfish. Its tentacles contain one of nature's strongest poisons.

 Twice the Fun!

Sea anemones can reproduce by tearing themselves in two. Each half then grows the new part it needs to repair itself.

This sea anemone is tearing itself in two.

Common Name	Scientific Name
jellyfish, sea anemones	*Coelenterata*

Double-Headers

Flatworms are, just as their name suggests, flat worms! Flatworms belong to the phylum of *Platyhelminthes* (say *platty-**hel**-minth-ees*). Some flatworms live on land or in the sea. Others, called **planaria**, live in streams.

Planaria have a simple brain that is *just* able to learn things. If a planaria is cut in two, its front end can grow a new back, and its back end can grow a new head. Each half can remember some of what it had learned before it was cut.

If a planaria's head is cut down the middle, each half repairs itself so that the planaria has two heads. Eventually, the animal may split completely in half to make two new planaria.

Tape-Measure Time!

Some flatworms—called tapeworms — can live in the intestines of humans. The longest tapeworm to live in humans is the broad fish tapeworm—which can grow over fifty feet long.

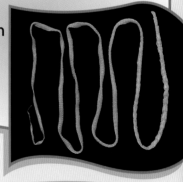

a tapeworm

Common Name	Scientific Name
flatworms	*Platyhelminthes*

All-Rounders

A ribbon worm is even longer than a tapeworm. Ribbon worms live in the ocean. They grow up to 180 feet long, which makes them the longest of all animals. Ribbon worms and roundworms belong to the phylum of *Nematodes* (say *nem-a-toads*).

Roundworms live in the soil and in water. Others live as **parasites** inside animals and plants. Although you don't often see roundworms, they are one of the most common animals on Earth.

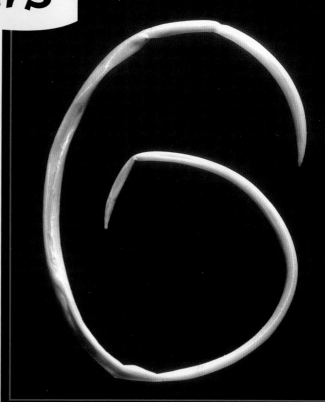

You don't often see roundworms, but they are one of the most common animals on Earth.

⊚ Picture This!

Roundworms live everywhere: in plants, animals, soil, and water. If you magically removed everything on Earth *except roundworms*, you would still see ghostly outlines of trees, animals, people, lakes, mountains and rivers.

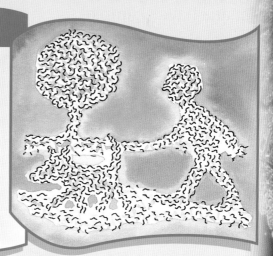

Common Name	Scientific Name
roundworms	*Nematoda*

Shell-Shockers

Some animals have a shell on the outside to protect them. These animals belong to the phylum of *Molluscs* (say *mol-usks*). Mussels, clams, snails, squid, and octopuses are all mollusks.

Snails in Love

Cupid searching for lovers

a snail searching for a mate

What does Cupid have in common with a snail? Cupid shot arrows into the hearts of people who fell in love (and that's why a heart with an arrow is the sign of love). Garden snails have a similar trick. Each snail is both male and female at the same time. Before mating, snails fire small darts into each other. The darts are shaped just like spear points.

One Big Happy Family!

How would you like twenty-five million brothers and sisters? If you were a mussel, you wouldn't have much choice! A mussel can squirt up to twenty-five million eggs into the sea in a single spawning.

How many in your family?

I'm the younges of 25,000,000

Outside-In Cuttlefish!

Most mollusks have their shells on the outside—except cuttlefish. A cuttlefish has its protective shell *inside* its body. The shell of a cuttlefish is full of air spaces. The air acts like the air tanks in a submarine and allows the cuttlefish to float. Cuttlefish shells often washes up on beaches as "cuttlebone."

Cuttlefish like to be different: they have their protective shells *inside* their bodies.

Hungry Clams

hungry clam

Animals use chemicals to digest their food. In most animals, these chemicals are liquids. A clam is different; it has a stiff chemical rod in its stomach. Tiny hairs spin the rod around, and its end turns against a small file, grating chemicals off the rod and into the clam's food.

Care for Some Squid?

A **kraken** is a giant squid. The largest kraken ever recorded was fifty-five feet long. Scientists believe that there are squid even bigger than this, because whales have been found with sucker marks the size of dinner plates on their skin.

A kraken is a giant squid.

Common Name	Scientific Name
mussels, clams, snails, cuttlefish, squid, octopuses	*Mollusca*

A Worm's-Eye View

An earthworm's "rings" show where each segment, or part, is joined.

There are lots of worms in the world, and some are more advanced than others. They belong to the phylum of *Annelids* (say **anna**-lids). Earthworms are among these most advanced worms.

An earthworm looks as though it has rings around its body. Its body is actually divided into a string of compartments, or **segments**, all of which are alike. The worm is built like a train with lots of cars, all of them the same. Only the segments toward the front of the body are different: they contain the worm's mouth, brain, and reproductive organs.

That Sinking Feeling!

Earthworms eat leaves and soil underground, then deposit their waste as worm castings on the surface. If they are well fed, they can lift the level of the soil about two inches in ten years. The rise in soil level has been enough to bury ancient buildings, which seem to sink slowly into the ground.

We'll have to stop feeding those worms!

Common Name	Scientific Name
earthworms	*Annelida*

Armor-Plated

Animals such as centipedes, insects, spiders, and crayfish have their skeletons outside their bodies. These skeletons are called **exoskeletons**, and they are like armor. Animals in this phylum are called *Arthropods* (pronounced *arth-ro-**pods***). About three-quarters of all animals on Earth are arthropods.

Smelly Ants

Ants might look as though they don't know where they're going, but they're really following scent trails.

Ants communicate by smell. Every time an ant finds food, it lays a chemical trail back to its nest. The other ants can then follow the trail to the food. When the food runs out, the ants stop laying the trail and the chemical evaporates.

Ants lay lots of other chemical messages. They lay trails that—

- identify who they are
- prevent too many queen ants from developing
- tell other ants to defend the nest

Somersaulting Flies

How do flies land on the ceiling? Do they roll over? Or do they fly upside down for a while? High-speed cameras show that flies actually do somersaults. As a fly moves toward the ceiling, it reaches up over its head with its forelegs. It then grabs the ceiling and flips the rest of its body up.

The Rafflesia flower attracts flies with its special aroma—rotting meat!

Flies do a somersault every time they land on the ceiling.

Yum! Rotting Meat!

Most flowers are brightly colored to attract insects. The insects feed from the flower's nectar and carry away the pollen. Plants that flower at night have strong scents so that insects can find them by smell, rather than by sight.

The world's largest flower is the Rafflesia; it looks and smells like rotting meat! Rafflesias don't attract bees and butterflies. They rely on flies to carry their pollen about.

👑 King Arthropod?

Henry the Eighth was King of England from 1509 to 1547. As King Henry grew fatter, he outgrew his suits of armor—they had to be made larger each time. It's the same with arthropods. As they grow, their "armor" becomes too small for them. Most of them regularly **shed** their armor to grow a bigger one.

It's time to buy a new exoskeleton!

It's Raining Blood!

In the Middle Ages, people were scared when it "rained blood." They thought it meant that disaster was coming. We now know that these rains were caused by butterflies.

Some butterflies drop "blood" when they hatch.

When some caterpillars grow into butterflies, they make a pale red liquid called **meconium**. When the butterflies hatch and fly off, each releases a drop of meconium—and it seems to be raining blood!

How Bees Beehive

Bees can't count—but they are good architects! Honeycomb is a collection of six-sided cells that share walls. This is the strongest structure you can make from the smallest amount of wax, and it also provides the greatest possible volume for honey storage.

Butterflies taste with their feet—it's lucky they don't wear shoes.

Feet First

Flies and butterflies taste with their feet. When they land on something good to eat, their mouth parts shoot out of their heads so that they can feed.

Every honeycomb cell is a hexagon.

Could you walk without tripping if you had as many legs as a centipede?

Cunning Running

A centipede does not have one hundred legs—as its name suggests—but it does have lots of legs. So, how does it avoid tripping over its own feet? Each set of legs is slightly longer than the set in front. As it runs, the back legs step slightly outside those in front of them.

An insect manages six legs without a problem, too. It moves its legs like two sets of tripods. The front and back legs of one side move with the middle leg of the other side. The insect then changes sides to use the other three legs in the same way.

Insect Olympics

Some insects are incredibly strong. A stag beetle can pull 120 times its own weight. This is like you dragging a 13,000-pound weight. An ant can raise fifty times its own weight.

Fleas are the best jumpers. A flea can jump thirteen inches, which is like you jumping over 300 feet!

A stag beetle can drag 120 times its own weight.

Common Name	Scientific Name
centipedes, insects, spiders, crustaceans	*Arthropoda*

Suckers

Starfish have suckers on their feet. Each sucker is filled with water.

Starfish, sea urchins, and sea cucumbers belong to the phylum of *Echinoderms* (say *ek-ine-o-derms*). Most echinoderms have spiny skins.

Echinoderms have hundreds of feet. Each foot is a small water-filled sucker.

Echinoderms can blow up their feet and attach them to rocks or shells. They can also use their feet to pull themselves along. Their feet are very special—no other animal has anything like them.

 Extra-Fast Food!

Many echinoderms don't have to eat their food to digest it. A starfish can push its stomach out through its mouth and digest a mussel within its own shell.

Dad! Emma's doing her starfish trick again!

Common Name	Scientific Name
starfish, sea urchins, sea cucumbers	*Echinodermata*

15

Spine-Tinglers

Animals with spines belong to the phylum of *Chordates* (say *kor-day-ts*). Fish, amphibians, reptiles, birds, and mammals are all chordates.

Fish

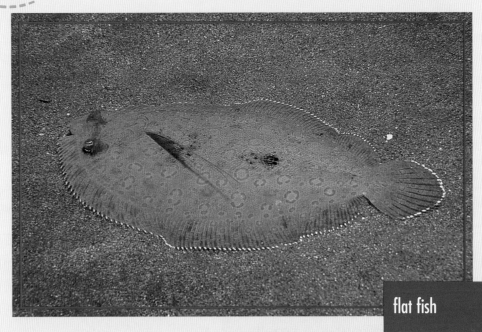

flat fish

A flat fish, such as a plaice or a flounder, starts life with an eye on each side of its head, like any other fish. But as it grows into an adult, one eye slowly moves around its body until both eyes are together on the same side. Adult flat fish lie on the sea floor on one side, with both eyes staring upward.

This Is My Other Brother...

A sunfish can lay up to 300 million eggs in one spawning. Just twenty sunfish could lay as many eggs as there are people on Earth.

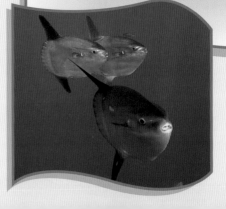

Baby sunfish always have other sunfish to play with.

Amphibians

Amphibians are animals that live on land and in water.

Gulp!

The bulging eyes of a frog look appealing, but they do more than just see. Frogs have no teeth, and they cannot chew. When a frog catches an insect, it uses its eyeball muscles to help crush the insect in its throat. The eyeball muscles then force the dead insect into the frog's stomach. That's why frogs close their eyes when they swallow.

Frogs use their powerful eye muscles to help them swallow.

☂ It's Raining Cats and Frogs!

Sometimes there are news reports of frogs or fish raining from the sky. These animals are sucked up from ponds and lakes by tornadoes, called **waterspouts**, that form over water. When the waterspout loses its energy, the frogs or fish are released...and fall to the ground like rain!

Reptiles

Reptiles are cold-blooded animals with scaly skin.

Deafening Silence

In India, snake charmers play tunes to "dancing" snakes. Snakes are totally deaf, but they are sensitive to vibrations. The snakes are actually "dancing" to the vibrations from the snake charmer's tapping foot.

This cobra is dancing to the snake charmer's music—or is it?

Snakes smell with their tongues. They flick their tongues in and out to gather particles from the air. Then they transfer the particles to their smell organs inside their mouths. The smell organs are like pockets on each side of a snake's mouth; each fork of the tongue fits into its own pocket.

A High-Fiber Diet

Crocodiles swallow stones for **ballast**. They keep the stones in their stomachs so they don't float on top of the water when their stomachs are empty. They swallow their **prey** whole or in large pieces.

If the prey is hairy, the hair is not digested. Instead, the hair is rolled into a dense hairball inside the crocodile's stomach and **regurgitated**, or spat out.

Crocodile Tears

When someone is pretending to be sad, it is said they are weeping "crocodile tears." Crocodiles don't actually cry, but they do have glands in the corners of their eyes that get rid of excess salt from their bodies. The salty liquid looks like tears.

Crocodiles' eyes have glands that get rid of excess salt.

Birds

Blurred Hummingbird

The hummingbird is the only bird that can fly backward. It beats its wings a fantastic ninety times a second.

The wings of a hummingbird beat an amazing ninety times per second.

Hummingbirds use up lots of energy. If a hummingbird were your size, it would need to eat forty-four times as much food as you do (which makes 132 meals a day) to still be able to fly.

The Tooth Truth

Something that is rare or unusual is "as rare as hens' teeth." This means it's really rare...because hens don't have teeth. But they do have one tooth, briefly. A chicken has to escape from its own eggshell. It has a tiny spur on the end of its beak, called an **egg tooth**. The chicken uses the egg tooth to crack its shell from the inside. The egg tooth disappears a few days after hatching.

A chicken briefly enjoys the use of its tooth.

Mammals

Mammals are warm-blooded animals that suckle their young on milk.

Sea Maids

Dugongs and manatees are mammals that live in the sea. They look a bit like seals, and have flippers instead of legs. Early sailors couldn't make out what they were. They invented the myth of the mermaid—a creature that was half-woman, half-fish—to explain what they saw.

dugong pretending to be a mermaid

Seeing Spots

The panther and the leopard are really the same animal. The panther is just a black version of the leopard. You can still see a panther's black spots because they have a different texture from the rest of its fur.

Stick Your Neck Out!

What do a mouse and a giraffe have in common? They both have seven bones in their necks! All mammals—no matter how tall they are—have seven bones in the neck part of their spines.

A panther is a black version of a leopard.

Big and Little

An African elephant is the largest land animal, but the blue whale is twenty times bigger. The blue whale is the largest animal that has ever lived. The biggest blue whale recorded was 98 feet long. It weighed more than 165 tons.

The blue whale is the largest of all animals.

The smallest mammal is the pygmy shrew, which weighs about one-fourth ounce.

Feeling Thirsty?

A camel does *not* store water in its hump. Instead, it stores fat. Camels are able to convert the stored fat into water. A camel's nose also acts like a **still**. On cold nights, moisture in a camel's breath is condensed into water inside its nose.

The largest land animal is the African elephant.

The pygmy shrew is the smallest mammal.

Camels have adapted to living in waterless places.

Common Name	Scientific Name
fish, amphibians, reptiles, birds, mammals	*Chordata*

Animal Relationships Tree

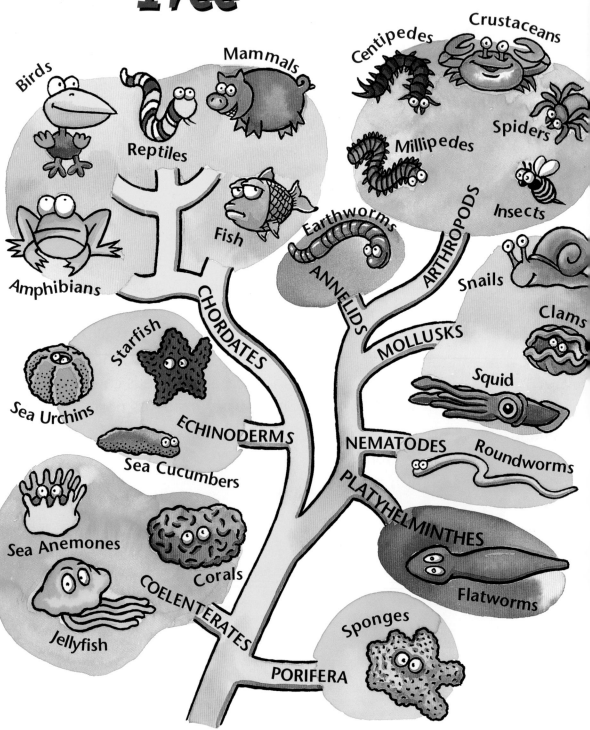

Glossary

amphibians   animals that live on land and in water

annelids   worms that have their bodies in segments

arthropods   animals that have their skeletons outside their bodies

ballast   weight used to keep an empty ship (or crocodile!) stable

chordates   animals with backbones; includes fish, amphibians, reptiles, birds, and mammals

coelenterates   animals with soft round bodies and no backbones

echinoderms   animals with spiky skins

egg tooth   the tiny spur on a baby bird's beak

exoskeleton   a skeleton on the outside of a body; body armor

kraken   a type of giant squid

mammals   warm-blooded animals that suckle their young on milk

meconium   liquid waste from a hatching butterfly

mollusks   animals with protective outer shells

nematodes   simple types of worm

parasites   animals that live on or in other animals

phylum   a group of animals that have the same features

planaria   a flatworm that lives in streams

plankton   microscopic plants and animals that live in oceans

platyhelminths   flatworms

porifera   the phylum name for sponges

predators   animals that hunt and kill other animals

prey   an animal that is hunted for food

regurgitate   to vomit

reptiles   cold-blooded animals with scaly skin

sea anemone   a relative of the jellyfish

segment   a part of something

shed   to leave behind; discard

still   a device for turning vapor back into water

tentacles   long, flexible feelers used for feeding and grasping

waterspout   a tornado that sucks up water

zoologists   people who study animals

Index